I0828196

THIS BOOK BELONGS TO:

WELCOME
TO INDIANA

Dedicated to all the explorers.

ISBN 978-1-958985-87-8

www.joeysavestheday.com

A Mimi Book

Indiana got its name because the land was once home to many Native American nations. The word "Indiana" simply means "Land of the Indians." When the United States created the Indiana Territory in the early 1800s, the name was chosen to honor the Native peoples who lived there long before it became a state.

Indiana's history begins with Native American nations such as the Miami, Potawatomi, and Shawnee. French explorers arrived in the 1600s and built trading posts throughout the region. After the American Revolution, the land became part of the Northwest Territory, and Indiana grew quickly as settlers moved west. Indiana became the 19th state in 1816. The state played an important role in farming, transportation, and industry, and today it is known for its manufacturing, its farmland, and the famous Indianapolis 500.

Indiana was the nineteenth state to join the Union. It officially joined on December 11, 1816.

19th

Indiana is located in the Midwestern region of the United States. It is bordered by Michigan, Ohio, Kentucky, and Illinois, and it also touches Lake Michigan.

Indianapolis is the capital of Indiana.
It officially became the capital in 1825.

Indianapolis, Indiana, has an estimated population of about 891,000 people.

There are approximately 6,924,000
people residing in the state of Indiana.
Bloomington, Indiana

Indiana is the thirty-eighth largest state in the United States by area.

Indiana

There are 92 counties in Indiana.

Here is a list of twenty of those counties:

Adams	Daviess	Hancock	Madison
Bartholomew	Delaware	Hendricks	Morgan
Boone	Floyd	Jasper	Posey
Cass	Gibson	Knox	Tippecanoe
Clark	Grant	LaGrange	Warrick

Madam C.J. Walker was born on December 23, 1867, in Louisiana and later built her successful hair-care business while living in Indiana. She created products that helped women care for their hair and became one of the first self-made female millionaires in America. Walker used her success to support schools, charities, and civil rights causes.

Let your light Shine

SUCCESS

DREAM BIG, WORK HARD, MAKE IT happen.

Thistlethwaite Falls is a wide, beautiful waterfall tucked along the Whitewater River in Richmond, Indiana. The falls were first shaped in the early 1800s when Timothy Thistlethwaite, a local mill owner, redirected part of the river to power his gristmill. Today, the waterfall spills over layers of ancient limestone, creating a curtain of rushing water. The rocks around the falls are full of fossils, so families often explore the riverbank looking for tiny shells and ancient sea creatures hidden in the stone.

The Indianapolis 500, often called the Indy 500, is one of the most famous car races in the world, and it takes place only in Indiana. Every year, drivers race 200 laps around the Indianapolis Motor Speedway, covering a total of 500 miles. The event began in 1911 and has become a major part of Indiana's history and identity. More than 300,000 people attend each year, making it one of the largest single-day sporting events on Earth.

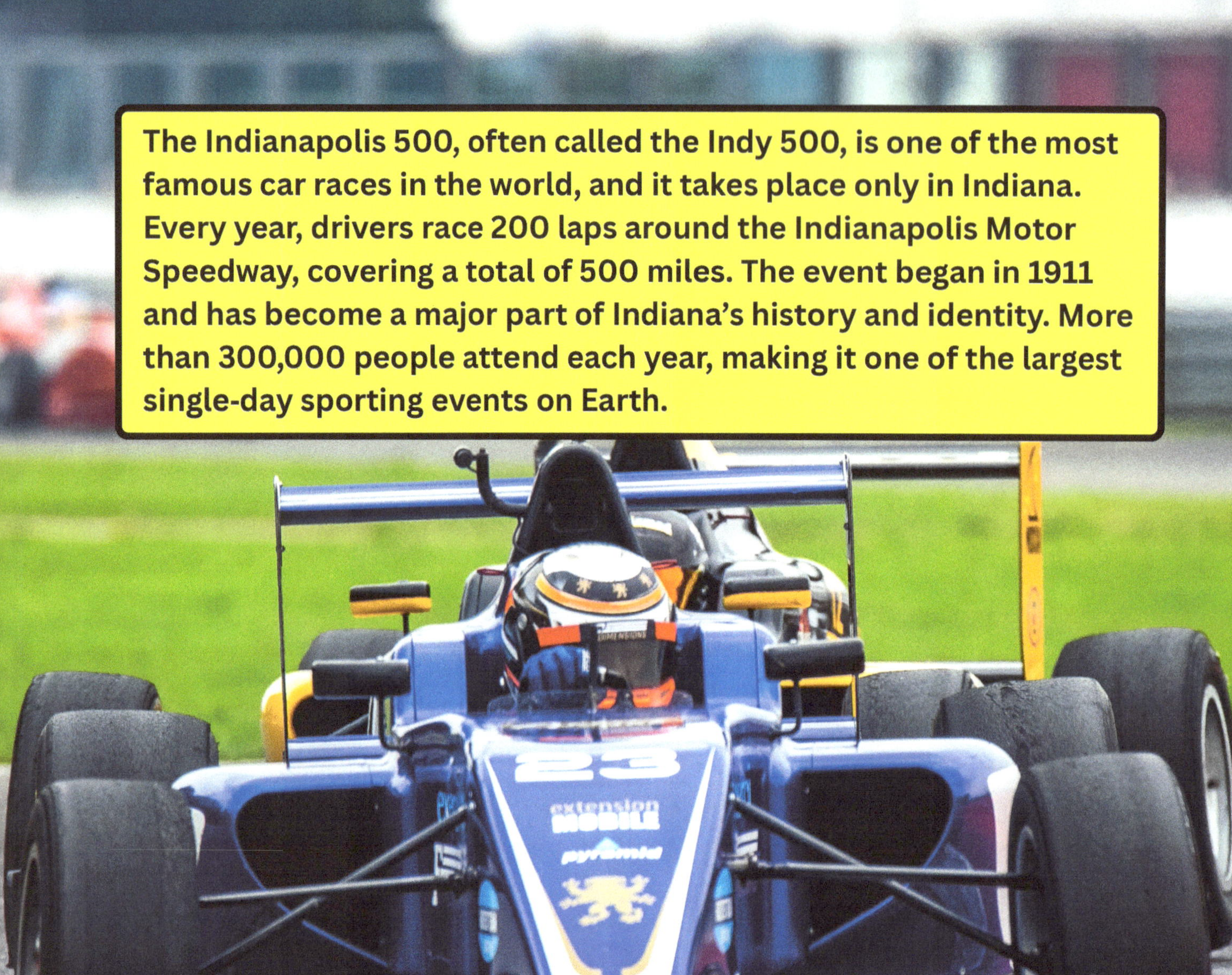

The George Rogers Clark Memorial Bridge connects Jeffersonville, Indiana, with Louisville, Kentucky, across the Ohio River. Opened in 1929, it is one of Indiana's most recognizable river crossings. The bridge is 5,746 feet long and carries both cars and pedestrians. It is named after George Rogers Clark, a Revolutionary War hero who helped secure the Northwest Territory.

Indiana is commonly referred to as the Hoosier State.

THE HOOSIER STATE!

Indiana's state motto is "The Crossroads of America." It became the official motto in 1937.

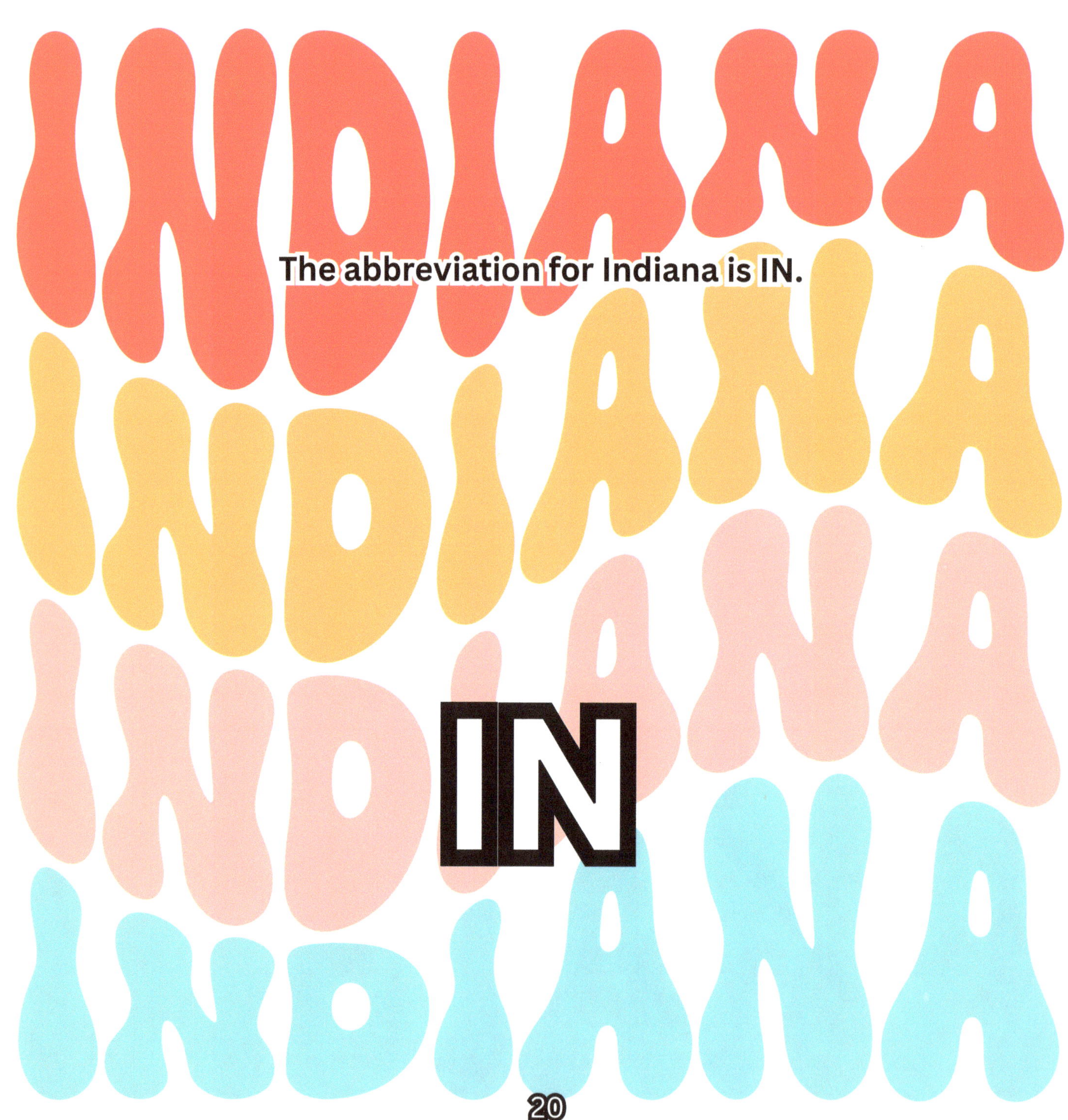

The abbreviation for Indiana is IN.

IN

Indiana's state flag was officially adopted in 1917.

Indiana is famous for its giant pork tenderloin sandwich, which is made by pounding a piece of pork very thin, breading it, and frying it until it's crispy and golden. The tenderloin is usually much bigger than the bun, which makes kids laugh when they see it hanging over the sides. It's a classic meal served at diners, fairs, and small hometown restaurants all across the state.

Some crops grown in Indiana are corn, soybeans, wheat, and tomatoes.

Indiana experiences wide temperature swings throughout the year. The hottest temperature ever recorded in the state was 116°F, measured in Collegeville on July 14, 1936. On the opposite end, Indiana's coldest temperature was −36°F, recorded in New Whiteland on January 19, 1994.

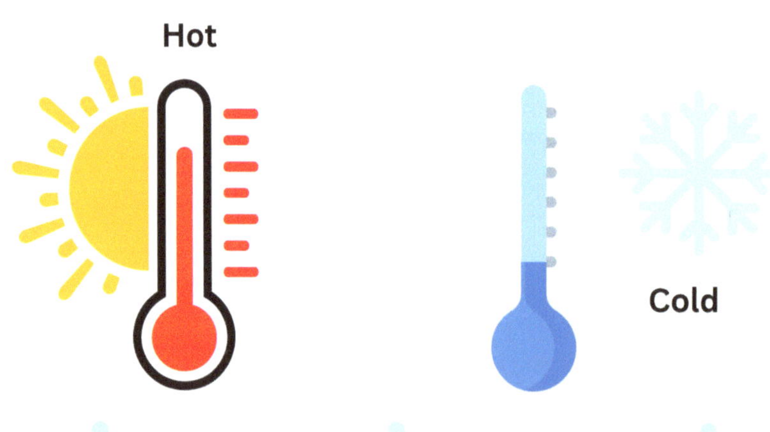

The largemouth bass is Indiana's state fish. It's a strong, sleek fish known for its quick bursts of speed and powerful jumps as it moves through Indiana's warm lakes and slow-moving rivers. Even though it's a skilled hunter, the largemouth bass is calm most of the time, gliding through underwater plants in search of smaller fish and insects.

The Indiana state bird is the Northern Cardinal.
It was chosen as the state bird in 1933.

Some animals that live in Indiana are white-tailed deer, red foxes, coyotes, bobcats, and great horned owls.

The Fort Wayne Children's Zoo in Fort Wayne is one of Indiana's most beloved places to learn about animals. Kids can meet creatures that live in and around the state, like river otters, ostriches, clouded leopards, and kangaroos, along with owls, hawks, and other colorful birds. The zoo highlights wildlife from Indiana and beyond, making it a fun place for families to explore nature together.

Indiana Dunes National Park is one of Indiana's most magical places, where sandy beaches, tall dunes, and peaceful forests all come together along the edge of Lake Michigan. Families can wander along miles of shoreline, hike through quiet woodlands, and explore rolling dunes shaped by the wind.

The largest airport in Indiana is Indianapolis International Airport, located in Indianapolis, near the center of the state. It sits at 7800 Col. H. Weir Cook Memorial Drive, Indianapolis, Indiana, and serves as the main travel hub for people flying in and out of Indiana. The airport connects travelers to cities all across the country and is known for its easy layout, friendly atmosphere, and bright, modern design.

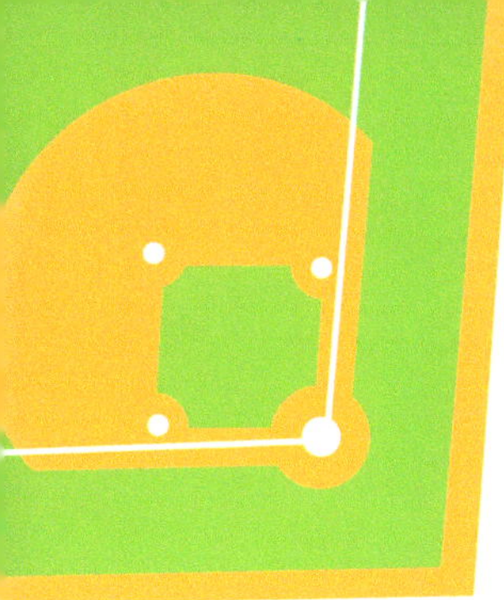

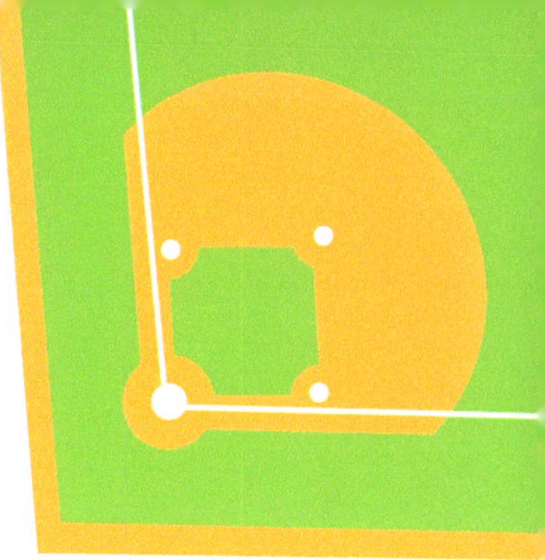

The Indianapolis Indians are a Minor League Baseball team located in the vibrant heart of Indianapolis. They host their home games at Victory Field, a lively and inviting ballpark celebrated for its family-friendly environment and stunning views of the downtown skyline.

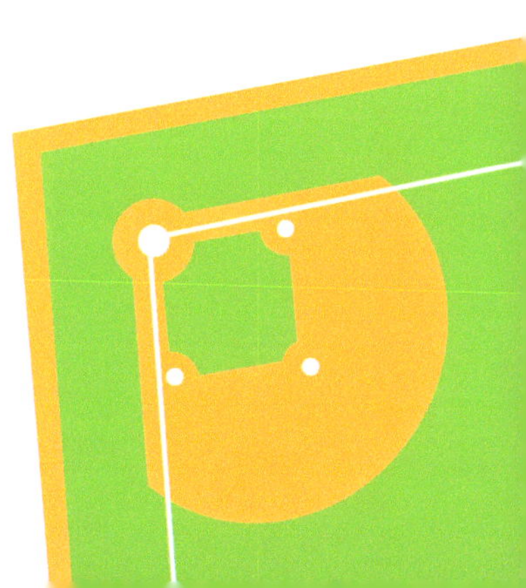

FOOTBALL

The Indiana Hoosiers are one of the most well-known football teams in the state, and they play in Bloomington, in the southern part of Indiana. Their home field is Memorial Stadium, a lively place where fans dress in cream and crimson to cheer on the team. The Hoosiers are known for their determined, energetic play and the strong sense of community that fills the stadium on game days, making each matchup feel like a true Indiana tradition.

The official state flower of Indiana is the Peony.
It was chosen as the state flower in 1957.

The tulip tree is Indiana's state tree. It stays leafy and bright through the warm seasons and grows tall and straight, giving Indiana's forests their peaceful, green canopy. Tulip trees have large, uniquely shaped leaves and beautiful yellow-green blossoms, and they've played an important role in Indiana's history. Their strong, lightweight wood was once prized for building cabins, barns, and furniture, helping early communities grow all across the state.

Can you name these?

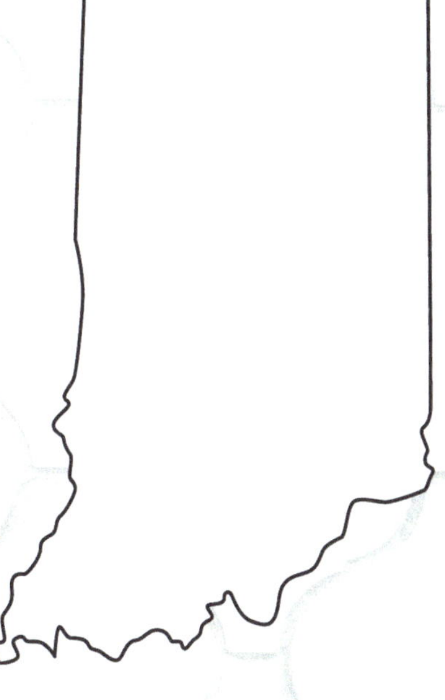

I hope you enjoyed
learning about
Indiana.

To explore fun facts about the other 49 states, visit my website at www.joeysavestheday.com. You'll also find a wide variety of homeschool resources to support joyful learning at home. If you enjoyed this book, I would be grateful if you left a review. Your feedback truly helps. Thank you for your support!

Check out these other interesting books in the 50 States Fact Books Series!

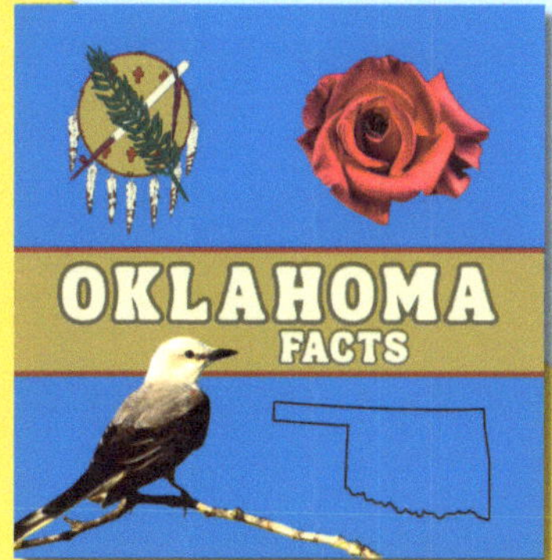

www.mimibooks.com

www.ingramcontent.com/pod-product-compliance
Lightning Source LLC
LaVergne TN
LVHW070200110826
845147LV00002B/454

9781958985878